SIKH STUDIES

BOOK 3

Guru Nanak Dev

Dr. H.S. Singha
Former
Principal, Guru Harkrishan Public School
Vasant Vihar, New Delhi
and
Chairman CBSE, New Delhi
Satwant Kaur

Trusted since 1948

NOTE FOR THE TEACHERS AND PARENTS

Understanding different religions and the basic elements underlying them, lays the foundation for a good human being. Such understanding must be imparted at an early age.

Keeping this in view, Sikh Public Schools in India have introduced religious instruction known as 'Sikh Studies' or 'Divinity' as a compulsory part of their curriculum. The present series has been developed to provide them a complete course in the subject upto the secondary stage.

The series is also aimed at meeting the needs of Sikh children settled abroad by giving them graded tools for study at home or in a Sunday school. This will also be a good resource material for use in summer camps for Sikh children studying in other schools.

THE SERIES CONSISTS OF THE FOLLOWING BOOKS:

Book I-II are meant as a launching pad for a study of Sikhism by junior children. They cover the basic facts about Sikhism for beginners. As reading skills are being developed at this stage, illustrations are profusely given to be used as a fulcrum. We also solicit the support of parents and teachers for imparting knowl-edge. Hints for them have been given at the end of each chapter.

Book III-V give *sakhis* or stories about the Sikh Gurus. They have become a part of the folklore in Punjab. They most effectively convey the teachings of Sikhism in a manner traditionally accepted in all religions.

Book VI gives similar *sakhis* or stories about the Sikh Heroes. It thus covers the post-Guru Gobind Singh period of Sikh history. In fact it carries Sikh history, from Banda Singh Bahadur to Maharaja Ranjit Singh.

Book VII is a formal culmination of the series for adolescent children. It intro-duces them formally to Sikh theology, ethics, psyche etc. after tracing the evolution of Sikhism.

Supplementary Book. It gives the complete ardaaswith pictorial cues for easy learning. The text is given in both Gurmukhi and Roman scripts with an English translation.

I have tried to keep the language as simple as possible. But there are obvious limitatios because of the nature of the subject matter. I hope that illustrations, will relieve this feature to some extent. Comments and suggestions for improvement are welcome.

- **Authors**

Printed at : Sita Fine Arts Pvt. Ltd., New Delhi

CONTENTS

1

LIFE SKETCH OF GURU NANAK DEV

Guru Nanak Dev is the founder of Sikhism and the first Guru of Sikhs.

He was born in 1469 AD at Talwandi. This place is now called Nankana Sahib and is situated in Pakistan.

The name of the Guru's father was Kalyan Chand which has been shortened by writers and others to Kalu. He was a Hindu Khatri. He was a village official called Patwari who is in general responsible for keeping the records. The Guru's mother was Tripta.

Guru Nanak Dev was sent for receiving instruction at the age of about six. Pandit Gopal taught him the local language, Pandit Brij Nath Sanskrit and Maulvi Kutubdin Persian. The Guru was different and out of the ordinary student. He had different interests. He was looking for deeper meanings in everything that was taught. He had no respect for traditions, customs and religious rites. He even questioned the sacred thread, *(Janeiu)* ceremony at the age of eleven.

As the Guru grew up, he was asked to take the cattle for grazing in the pasture. He was not interested in worldly affairs. He would spend his solitude for inward communion. His father wanted him to enter business but he preferred to spend the money on hungry mendicants *(Sadhus)*

At the age of fifteen, Guru Nanak Dev was sent to his sister Bibi Nanaki at Sultanpur Lodhi, a small ancient town 25km from Kapurthala on the bank of a rivulet *(Bein)*. There he took up the job of the storekeeper of the Nawab named Daulat Khan Lodhi. The Guru was however more interested in spiritual work. This sometimes clashed with his official work and led to controversies. It was while at Sultanpur that he got married and had two sons: Sri Chand and Lakhami Chand.

Once, when at Sultanpur, the Guru went for the morning bath at the rivulet. He did not return for three days. Everybody was worried.

But the Guru was having the mystical experience. When he appeared after three days he was uttering loudly "One is neither a Hindu nor a Muslim" This became the first tenet of Sikhism. Indeed the Guru was ready to preach the message of universal brotherhood.

Guru Nanak Dev left Sultanpur Lodhi in 1497 AD with his constant companion Mardana on his first missionary travel. This was followed later on by a few more such journeys to far off places. He covered most of India, Pakistan, Bangladesh and also went to Sri Lanka, Saudi Arabia, Iraq, Iran and Afganistan.

For the last few years, the Guru settled down at Kartarpur (Pakistan) on the banks of river Ravi as a householder. Here he demonstrated the practice of Sikhism and became very popular. Before he passed away in 1539 AD, Sikhism had taken firm roots.

The stories which follow are important incidents in the life of Guru Nanak Dev. Since the Guru was leading the life of a true Sikh, they also provide meaning and interpretation of Sikhism. They are popularly called Sakhies and are a part of Punjabi folk lore.

2

TRUE   LEARNING

Guru Nanak Dev went for schooling at the age of about six. He learnt the local language from Pandit Gopal, Sanskrit from Pandit Brij Nath and Persian from Maulvi Kutubdin. The Guru was an out of the ordinary student. He was looking for much deeper understanding of things around him than a normal student would do. He talked of God and philosophy. His teachers took him to be a born messenger or prophet.

Once the teacher asked the Guru to write the alphabet on the wooden slate (Patti). He did so alright. At the same time, he gave a meaning to each letter of the alphabet.

When the Guru went to Pandit Brij Nath for learning Sanskrit, he asked him: "Brij Nath is the name of Lord Krishna. Sir, how is it your name as well?" The teacher was surprised. He had no answer. Later the Guru went on asking him more questions. The teacher asked him to keep quiet saying: "You are too young to know all these things." However, Guru Nanak Dev was not satisfied. His aim was true learning which is learning with full understanding. He proclaimed "Learning without understanding is not good. It is like groping in the dark." Better know nothing than half-know many things.

3

CUSTOMS AND RITES

According to Hindu customs and traditions, every devout Hindu is required to wear the sacred thread (Janeiu). Brahmins use three–ply thread; Kshatriyas two–ply; Vaishas one–ply and Shudras have no right to wear it.

The ceremony was held for Guru Nanak Dev when he was nine years old. According to the custom, all the relations were assembled to watch the ceremony. Pandit Hardyal was the master of ceremonies.

During the ceremony, Pandit Hardyal asked the Guru to bow his head before an idol. The Guru asked: "Why is it necessary to do it?" The Pandit explained, "Because it is Lord Vishnu – the Preserver of the world." "But dear Pandit, how can a stone sculpture be the Lord ?" insisted the Guru.

When Pandit Hardyal tried to put the sacred thread on the Guru, he again protested. He asked the Pandit many pointed questions. "Why is it necessary to put on the sacred thread? What is the use? What do I lose if I don't wear it?" Obviously the Pandit had no answers except : "This is a Hindu custom." Guru Nanak Dev was not convinced. He was against all purposeless customs and rites.

14

4

TRUE TRADING

When Guru Nanak Dev grew somewhat older, his father Kalu wanted him to go into trading. He started sending the Guru to the nearby town of Chuharkana to trade in common salt.

One day Guru Nanak Dev left Talwandi with some money for

Chuharkana. There he met a group of Sufi saints. They were hungry. The Guru got the urge to feed them. So he spent the whole amount on their food rather than doing trading. The

gurdwara Sacha Sauda has been built at the place where the Guru had distributed food to the Sufi saints.

When Guru Nanak Dev returned to Talwandi on that day, he sat outside the town for some time. His father met him there and rebuked him for negligence. At that place, the gurdwara named Tamboo Sahib, exists now.

In the eyes of Guru Nanak, charity was one of the highest values. Feeding the hungry was more important than making money through trade.

5

"TERA!   TERA!"

Sultanpur Lodhi is a small ancient town 25 km from Kapurthala. It is situated on the left bank of the rivulet – Bein. At the time of Guru Nanak Dev, it was a great centre of Muslim culture. It was then ruled by Nawab Daulat Khan Lodhi.

The store of the Nawab was not well managed. There were many complaints. The Nawab was on the look out for a good storekeeper.

The Guru's sister Bibi Nanaki was at Sultanpur. Through her husband, the Guru was employed as the Nawab's storekeeper in 1484 AD. He spent nearly fourteen years here. He was, however, never at ease with his worldly duties. He was always yearning for the spiritual experience.

As a part of his duties as a storekeeper, the Guru had to weigh grain in ordinary scales involving counting. In this process, whenever he reached thirteen *(tera)*, he would go on repeating "tera! tera!" in a trance without stopping weighing but won't go beyond 13. The result was that a lot of grain was distributed to customers without any proper account.

The news reached the Nawab, who ordered an enquiry. However, the enquiry by Munshi Jado Rai revealed that in fact the store owed Rs. 321 to Guru Nanak Dev. The amount was duly paid. But the Guru distributed it among the poor.

The mystique of the sound of "tera!"which means "I belong to you ! Everything belongs to you!" had in it the hidden message of Sikhism about the relationship between God and man. God is all supreme. Everything in this universe belongs to Him.

6

UNIVERSAL BROTHERHOOD

Guru Nanak Dev had finally decided to give up his service as a storekeeper at Sultanpur. He had got the divine call to spread the spiritual message.

One day, the Guru went out in the early morning for his daily bath at the rivulet (Bein). He did not return home for three days. Everybody was worried. He might have been drowned in the rivulet. Or, he might have been eaten up by a crocodile. It was only his sister Bibi Nanaki who was sure that the Guru was alive and would come back.

So it happened. The Guru appeared in the streets of Sultanpur Lodhi on the fourth day. Although it was a Muslim state, the Guru was fearlessly uttering-rather loudly - "One is neither a Hindu nor a Muslim."

The fanatic Muslims complained to Nawab Daulat Khan Lodhi. They asked him to take strong action against the Guru. The Nawab summoned the Guru to the court to explain what he meant by saying: "One is neither a Hindu nor a Muslim."

The Guru gave a simple but beautiful explanation. "It is only the body which may be called Hindu or Muslim. All of us have, however, the same soul." This was, indeed, the first formal

message of Guru Nanak. It is a message of universal brotherhood – a message for loving each other.

7

TRUE WORSHIP

The pronouncement by Guru Nanak Dev at Sultanpur Lodhi : "One is neither a Hindu nor a Muslim" was too radical. It could not go unquestioned – much less by the Muslim priests close to Nawab Daulat Khan.

The Qazi of Sultanpur asked Guru Nanak Dev : "If one is neither a Hindu nor a Muslim – and all are the same – why don't you come with us for Namaz (Muslim Prayer) ?" The Guru readily agreed to accompany the Nawab and Qazi to the mosque. The town was agog with rumours. People thought that Guru Nanak Dev was being converted into a Muslim in the mosque. But he

had an entirely different mission.   He wanted to preach the meaning of true worship.

When the Namaz started, the head priest of the mosque and the Nawab along with others present bowed to pray. Guru Nanak Dev, much to the surprise of everyone, did not join them.

At the end of the Namaz, the Nawab asked the Guru the reason for the discourtesy. He had willingly come all the way to the mosque but had not cared to join in worship.

Guru Nanak Dev replied : "Sorry! When you bowed for prayers, your mind was not in God. You were actually thinking of purchasing horses in Kabul. Similarly the head priest was all the time worried that the new born colt in his stable may not have fallen into the well. You were only performing a ritual. It was not a real worship." He further elaborated that it is better not to pray when the mind is wandering about worldly things.

Nawab Daulat Khan was surprised at the revelations. He, however, accepted the advice of the Guru.

8

BREAD OF HARD WORK

After spending 14 years at Sultanpur Lodhi, Guru Nanak Dev started on his first missionary travel. He passed through many villages and towns. He touched places where are now situated Goindwal and Taran Tarn. He also went to Dipalpur and Lahore.

The Guru spent 20 days at Lahore. Then he reached Saidpur. There lived a poor, low caste carpenter whose name was Lalo. The Guru was impressed by his simplicity and hard work. He became Guru's disciple. And, one day he invited the Guru for meals. The Guru gladly accepted the invitation and joined the family for meals.

The high caste Hindus of the town were shocked. They started criticizing Guru Nanak Dev for his association with Lalo. Even, Malik Bhago one of the senior officials of the Ruler of Saidpur, planned to humiliate the Guru. He sent an invitation to the Guru for sumptuous meals prepared according to the requirements of caste system. The Guru declined the invitation. This made Malik Bhago very angry as he felt insulted. He asked the Guru the reason for not attending his dinner. Guru Nanak Dev gave him an answer which rather surprised him: "Lalo's bread earned by hard work is sacred food for me. Your dishes smell of corruption and blood."

The story goes to the extreme. Guru Nanak Dev gave a demonstration of what he meant. He called for food from the houses of Lalo and Bhago. Then he squeezed them in his hands. Lalo's food yielded milk while Bhago's food yielded blood.

9

AGAINST   SUPERSTITIONS

During his travels, Guru Nanak Dev reached Hardwar from his native village Talwandi.

Hardwar is a well-known centre of pilgrimage for Hindus. It is situated in Uttar Pradesh on River Ganga. It was the occasion of Baisakhi when Guru Nanak Dev reached there. Thousands of people had come to Hardwar for the annual fair.

It was morning time. The Guru had gone to River Ganga to

take bath. He saw many people throwing water upwards towards the East. The Guru started throwing water speedily towards the West.

Watching this, the bathers were surprised. They gathered around Guru Nanak Dev. One of them made bold and asked : "Why are you throwing water to the West ?" The Guru asked a counter question: "Why are you throwing it to the East ?" "Because, we are sending it to our forefathers" he replied. The Guru asked again, "How far are your forefathers ?" When told that they must be millions of kilometers away, the Guru started throwing water with still greater speed. He said : "I come from a village near Lahore which is to the West. It has not rained there much this year; so I am trying to water my fields." The bathers laughed at it. The Guru said: "Why are you laughing ? If your water can reach millions of kilometers, why can't my water reach near Lahore? It is less than 700 kilometers from here."

By saying so, Guru Nanak Dev had conveyed a deep message. It is not wise to believe blindly in superstitions or to follow meaningless rituals.

10

GREED MAKES SWEET THINGS BITTER

During his travels, Guru Nanak Dev had spent quite some time in Garhwal area.   He visited many places there, namely Srinagar (Garhwal), Badrinath, Ranikhet and Pilibhit.

During these days, the Guru was passing through a jungle. It is a spot about 50 km from where is now situated Gurdwara Nanakmata.   His constant companion Mardana felt desperately hungry. When he was unable to bear the pangs of hunger, the Guru asked him to pluck the fruit from a nearby soapnut (Reetha) tree.

"How can I take that fruit which is bitter and poisonous?" questioned Mardana.

The Guru said, " I'll also join you. I am sure they will be sweet." They were really so. Mardana enjoyed the fruit. But he became greedy. He took some more fruit from the tree for future needs. And he ate that fruit after some time when he again felt hungry. To his surprise the fruit was so bitter that he could not eat it. Guru Nanak Dev, advised him: "Never be greedy. Greed makes sweet things bitter".

The spot has become the famous Gurdwara Reetha Sahib.

11

ON GOOD COMPANY

From Garhwal Hills, Guru Nanak Dev had plans to go to the South. On his way he visited Allahabad, Ayodhya, Varanasi and Gaya. On his way to Patna Sahib from there, the Guru stayed at a village named Akbarpur.

There were two shopkeepers at Akbarpur. Both would close there shops at the same time in the evening. Then one would go to a life of sin with a prostitute. The other would go to Satsang.

One day they were discussing their experiences in the evening. The first said that on his return from the prostitute, he found a gold coin. The second narrated that on his return from Satsang,he got a thorn stuck in his foot.

The shopkeepers were unable to explain why did it happen the way it did. Since the Guru was in the village, they went to him to seek explanation. The Guru took them to the two spots and asked them to dig up there.

When the first spot where the gold coin was found was dug up, they hit a vessel full of burnt coal. Guru Nanak Dev said: "This is what happens with sin. It burns up the jewel of life and converts it into coal."

When the second spot was dug up, they found a hole with snakes in it. The snakes, however, withdrew into the hole. The

Guru explained: "Good company, particularly company of saints drives away all vices." It is because of Satsang that the shopkeeper was not bitten by the snakes.

12

IMPORTANCE OF INSIGHT

Guru Nanak Dev reached Patna Sahib. Here he found a diamond on the bank of River Ganga. He sent Mardana to the market to find out its price. The vegetable seller offered one radish; woodcutter four logs of wood; draper two metres of cloth; and confectioner half a kilo of sweets.

When Mardana went to Jeweller Salis Rai, he gave him Rs.100 for just looking at the diamond. He felt that it was indeed a rare thing which only the lucky persons could see. The Guru, however, returned the money. But he had demonstrated the importance of insight into things around us. It is insight which makes the difference between stone and diamond. Insight comes through training and education and by God's grace.

13

REFORMING A THIEF

From Patna Sahib, Guru Nanak Dev moved to the eastern parts of the country covering areas which are now called Bihar, West Bengal and Bangladesh. In the beginning of the 16th century, this area was infested with thieves, robbers and tricksters.

During his travels in that area, the Guru met a thief named Bhoomia. The Guru advised him to give up stealing. He, however, declined saying it was impossible. Then the Guru told him : "If you can't give up stealing, at least follow three instructions. One, always speak the truth; Two, don't cheat a person who has been good to you; and Three, don't rob a poor person." Bhoomia agreed to it.

Once Bhoomia organised a theft at the palace of the Rajah. Since he had promised to speak the truth he presented himself before the Rajah. As a result, he became a reformed person.

14

LET THE GOOD BE SCATTERED

When still travelling through Bengal, Guru Nanak Dev passed through a village. For no reason the villagers started throwing stones at the Guru. He, however, blessed them saying: "May you never be uprooted from your village." And, he carried on his journey.

When the Guru reached the next village the residents showed utmost respect. They joined him in the Shabad Kirtan as well.

When the Guru was leaving he said : "May you be uprooted from your village." This looked like a curse.

Mardana was surprised. He asked the Guru : "Why did you bless the bad not to be uprooted and curse the good people to be uprooted?"

The Guru explained : "The bad people are like disease for the society. They should be contained at one place. The good are like sandalwood fragrance. They must scatter."

15

EXPOSING AN EXPLOITER

After Bengal, Guru Nanak Dev toured North–Eastern states of Assam, Nagaland and Manipur. On his return from there via Calcutta and Burdwan he reached Puri - a town in Orissa famous for the Vishnu temple.

In Puri, there lived a Sadhu who used to cheat his devotees. He had spread the word that he could see heaven by closing his eyes. If any one wanted to reserve his seat in heaven, he could do so by putting some money in the jar kept before him.

The Guru watched this scene for some time. Then he decided to expose the Sadhu. He removed the jar in front of the Sadhu when he closed his eyes. He quietly put it behind him. Obviously the Sadhu could not discover it till he opened his eyes.

"How can you see what is going on in heaven when you can't see the jar being removed from your front?" asked the Guru.

The devotees present there were impressed. So was Rajah Krishan Lal of the region when he came to know of it.

16

STORY OF NANAK JHEERA

From Puri, Guru Nanak Dev went as far as Sri Lanka. On his return from there, he passed through Kerala, Tamil Nadu, Karnataka and Andhra Pradesh. He reached a place near Bidar in Karnataka.

There lived two Muslim *Pirs* : Said Yaqoob and Jalaludin. They had established complete sway in that area. They had controlled a spring of water by erecting walls around it. Since there was scarcity of water in that area, people were forced to visit their place and show respect for their creed.

The Guru camped outside their compound and started the

Shabad Kirtan. As it happened, there appeared a spring close-by. The one inside started drying up.

The Muslim Pirs were angry. They came out and started arguing with the Guru. He, however, counselled them about justice, mercy and devotion.

The place is now known as Nanak Jheera. A gurdwara has been constructed there.

17

ON VEGETARIANISM

Guru Nanak Dev was returning from his trip to South India. He passed through Indore, Ujjain, Dwarka and Delhi.

When he reached Kurukshetra, it was the time for the solar eclipse. Thousands of people had come there from all over the country for the fair. They were there to have a dip in the sacred tank. According to Hindu beliefs it is not considered right to do any work during the duration of the solar eclipse. Even the fire places for cooking (chulha) remain cool.

The Guru did not believe in all this. He not only lighted the fire, but started cooking a hunted deer presented to him. This was quite revolting for the pilgrims at Kurukshetra.

Guru Nanak Dev explained to Pandit Nanoo who was leading the group. "Planets are not influenced by our stoppage of work. Even eating meat does not make one pure or impure. In Hinduism, meat has been offered as sacrifice to deities since time immemorial."

Pandit Nanoo was convinced of the arguments.

[It may be pointed out that traditionally food served in Langars is vegetarian although Sikhs may take non-vegetarian food elsewhere].

41

18

ENCOUNTER WITH ASCETICS

Sidhi Sadhus are a sect of ascetics. They generally live on high mountains. They believe that salvation can be sought by torturing the body.

Guru Nanak Dev was a constant traveller. After covering far flung areas in the plains of India including Bangladesh and Sri Lanka, he left Sultanpur once again. This time he went to important places in the Himalayan Hills : Palampur, Kangra, Jawalamukhi, Ravalsar, Gangotri, Yamanotri etc.

While travelling in the hills, the Guru met a group of ascetics

led by Gorakh Nath. They were in the first instance surprised to see the Guru at an altitude of 6000 metres. They wanted to humble him in a debate on philosophy of life. This they could not do. Guru Nanak Dev had better arguments.

Ultimately they decided to impress him with their power to do miracles. They gave the Guru an empty bowl and asked him to fill it with water from the nearby tank. The Guru went there but came back empty-handed. He did not look for anything else even though diamonds and pearls were lying there.

The Guru said : "Sorry! There is no water there." They retorted: "Did you not see pearls and diamonds there ?" They were ashamed to hear the Guru say : "I had gone there looking for water. I had nothing to do with diamonds" They became his disciples

19

SOME ANGRY ASCETICS

All the groups of *Sidhi Sadhus* were not however converted. Guru Nanak Dev reached Ladakh after his encounter with Gorakh Nath and his followers. There some ascetics who were angry at the developments threw a rock at him. The rock, however, did not harm the Guru. It just touched his back.

A gurdwara is under construction at the site.

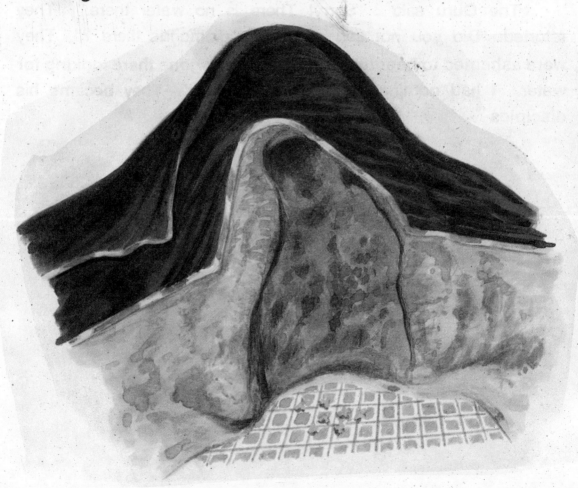

20

ON WISE PERSONS

After his trip to the Himalayan Hills, Guru Nanak Dev returned to Sialkot. He found the residents panicky. One fakir named Hamza Gons had undertaken 40 days fast. He was proclaiming that he would destroy the town with his powers after that period. Reason : One person had been false to his promise.

The Guru took a position outside the cave where the fakir was fasting. And, he started loud recitation of Shabad Kirtan. Hamza came out. The Guru tried to convince him by saying : "If

one person has been false, it does not mean everybody is bad. There are many good people in Sialkot who understand life."

To prove his point, the Guru sent Mardana to the market saying "Go there and buy Truth worth one Paisa and Falsehood worth one Paisa." Many people laughed at the idea. One trader Bhai Moola, however, accepted the deal. He gave Mardana two pieces of paper for one Paisa each. They were rolled as packets. Guru Nanak Dev opened them before Hamza. On the one was written "Death is the Truth" and on the second "Life is Falsehood." The Guru then explained its meaning. This convinced Hamza that Sialkot had still some wise people. He gave up his fast.

21

SAJJAN THUG

Guru Nanak undertook his long missionary journey to Muslim shrines in the Middle East. On his way to the Middle East, he stayed at a small town Tulambha in Pakistan.

In that town there lived an uncle-nephew team of thugs. One of them was named Sajjan. He had a nephew called Kajjan. They were very crafty. They were running an inn where they used to rob unwary travellers at night. The method was simple. Kajjan

would solicit the travellers to the inn. Sajjan would rob the rich ; make them unconscious by the smell of some herbs; and would then murder them. Sajjan used to plan the murders so well that no one could discover them. Indeed, those who were not robbed used to praise them for the arrangements.

Guru Nanak Dev also stayed at Sajjan's inn. He was shown normal courtesies. But Sajjan had his plans of robbing the Guru. When he did not go to sleep till late at night, Sajjan came to request him to retire. The Guru pleaded that he would do so after reciting one Shabad. This Shabad affected Sajjan so much that he became Guru's disciple.

22

SPIRIT OF KINDNESS

This story also relates to Guru Nanak Dev's missionary journey to the Middle East. Guru Nanak Dev stayed at a town called Bulani in Pakistan.

In that town lived a very skilled weaver named Dawood. He presented the Guru with a beautiful hand-woven carpet. He also requested the Guru to use it for his Shabad Kirtan.

The Guru preferred to do the Shabad Kirtan on a grassy lawn. So he politely declined. But Dawood left the carpet with the Guru.

At night Guru Nanak Dev heard the young pups of a bitch yelping and shivering with cold. The Guru put the carpet on them to give them warmth.

Guru Nanak Dev had demonstrated that we should have a kind heart. It is of no use looking after our own comforts if the living beings around us are suffering.

23

GURU NANAK DEV AT MECCA

Guru Nanak Dev reached Mecca via Aden. It is the holiest of the holy places for Muslims. They believe that at least once in their life time they must perform Haj by visiting Mecca. This is situated in Saudi Arabia and has the Great Mosque enclosing the Kaaba.

Guru Nanak Dev reached there at the time of annual Haj. The place was crowded with lacs of Muslim pilgrims from all over the world.

At night the Guru was sleeping in the great Mosque. His feet were pointing towards Kaaba. This orientation is not considered to be proper by Muslims.

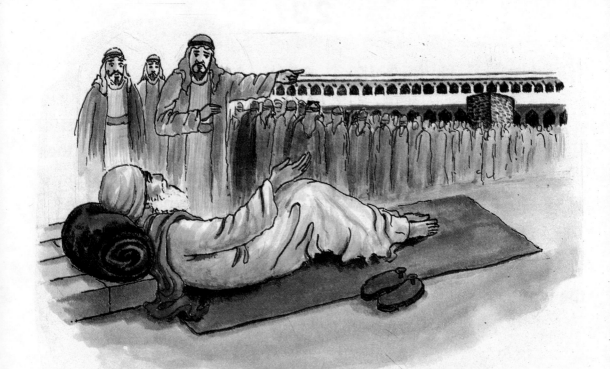

When the sweeper came in the morning to clean the area, he was shocked to see Guru Nanak Dev's feet towards Kaaba. He caught hold of the Guru's legs and turned his feet away from Kaaba. But he got a strange feeling as if Kaaba was moving in the direction of Guru's feet. He immediately proclaimed: "God's house is in no particular direction" This was the message, Guru Nanak Dev wanted to convey.

24

POWER OF SHABAD KIRTAN

From Mecca, Guru Nanak Dev moved on to Medina along with other Haj pilgrims. Medina is also an important pilgrim town in Saudi Arabia about 350 km from Mecca. Prophet Mohammed's tomb is situated there.

Guru Nanak Dev started the Shabad Kirtan outside the tomb. The pilgrims got angry. They started throwing stones at the Guru. He, however, did not stop the Shabad Kirtan. On the other hand, he raised the pitch higher repeating *"Akal! Akal!"*

The devotion with which the Guru was reciting ShabadKirtan moved the pilgrims. They threw away their stones. Their action changed. Their minds – which were the sources of actions – had been influnced by Shabad Kirtan.

25

PRIDE OF WALI KANDHARI

While returning from Mecca via Iraq, Guru Nanak Dev stayed at Hasan Abdal for some time. This is a place about 50 km from Rawalpindi in Pakistan. There was a Buddhist Monastry here. Its remains still exist.

Guru Nanak Dev had become very popular at Hasan Abdal. At that time, there also lived a Muslim saint named Wali Kandhari on a hill top. He was supposed to have healing powers. He became very jealous of the Guru's popularity. He started harassing the public, since the source of water was within his abode, he stopped the supply of water.

The Guru sent Mardana with a request for releasing the water. "Let your Guru provide water to the public", he shouted.

Guru Nanak Dev asked Mardana to search for a water spring outside the abode of Wali Kandhari. He requested him to try at the foot of the hill by removing some stones. Luckily, water gushed out in the form of a spring.

Wali Kandhari became still more angry. He rolled down a big rock on the Guru's camp. The Guru stopped it with his own hand which left an imprint on it. The rock still exists. A gurdwara called Panja Sahib was built there by Hari Singh Nalwa.

26

IMPORTANCE OF WORK

Finally Guru Nanak Dev completed his missionary travels. In old age he settled down with his family at Kartarpur (Pakistan). He had founded this town on the bank of River Ravi. He took to farming and lived the life of a perfect house–holder.

One day the Guru was working in the fields and was smeared with dust. Some of his companions were cutting wood. Others were busy cooking food. At that time, a group of Sadhus passed that way. On surveying the scene, they said, "Are you breeding animals here?" The Guru did no't get angry. He asked them to stay for a few days to find out for themselves. On watching everybody working they remarked after some days "You have many hard - working men on the farm." The Guru requested them to stay a little longer for final impression. After a few days more they said : "You have indeed devtas on the farm." He still insisted that they should stay longer. Finally they proclaimed. "These workers are, indeed the image of God."

27

CARING FOR OTHER'S NEEDS

At Kartarpur (Pakistan), the followers of Guru Nanak Dev were really practising all his teachings.

One day the Guru was going from his house to the fields. On the way, he saw one of his disciples shifting grain from one heap to the other. "What are you trying to do here?" asked the Guru. He got the reply: "We are two brothers. The grain was equally distributed into two heaps. However, my brother's need is greater.

He has a bigger family. I want him to get some more grain". The Guru blessed him and went on.

When Guru Nanak Dev returned after some time, he saw the other brother there. He was hastily shifting grain from his heap to that of his brother. "What are you doing here?" asked the Guru. He replied, "My brother gets lot of guests. The grain has been equally divided. But my brother's need is greater. I want him to get a little more grain. I am doing it hastily so that he does not turn up to stop me from doing so." Guru Nanak Dev blessed him also. This is how a true Sikh should feel and act.

28

THE GLORIOUS END

The teachings and practice of Sikhism had become very popular. Kartarpur (Pakistan) was a centre of pilgrimage. Large number of both Hindus and Muslims used to visit it. Indeed, the Guru was equally popular among both the communities.

When Guru Nanak Dev passed away in 1539 AD, both Hindus and Muslims wanted to perform the last rites according to

their own customs.   Either group claimed that the Guru belonged to it more than to the other.

The dispute was resolved peacefully.   They decided to have separate memorials according to their own traditions but with a common wall.   Hindus built a Samadhi;   the Muslims had a tomb. This joint memorial was later washad away in floods.

According to many historians, this is the only example of its kind in history.

REINFORCEMENTS

A. ORAL

1. Give the names of the following relations of Guru Nanak:
   (a) Father
   (b) Mother
   (c) Sister
   (d) Wife
   (e) Brother-in-law (Sister's husband)
2. The birth place of Guru Nanak is now known as Nankana Sahib. What was its original name ?
3. In which year was Guru Nanak born ? How many years long back was it ?
4. Give the names of three teachers of Guru Nanak.
5. Name three important *gurdwaras* at Nankana Sahib.
6. Name three important towns in India associated with Guru Nanak.
7. Name three important towns in Pakistan associated with Guru Nanak.
8. Give the names of three of the foreign countries visited by Guru Nanak during his travels.
9. The name of Guru Nanak's elder son was Sri Chand. What was the name of the younger son ?
10. At what place did Guru Nanak get his mystical experience or enlightenment?
11. Name two important *gurdwaras* in Q.No.10.
12. At what place did Guru Nanak settle down in old age to practise Sikhism ?
13. What is the importance of Dera Baba Nanak ?
14. The first words of Guru Nanak after his mystical experience were: "One is neither a Hindu, nor a Muslim ." What did he imply by it ?
15. Guru Nanak taught that "God is one." Does it mean that Sikhs, Hindus, Muslims and Christians have the same God ?
16. Recite Mul Mantra.
17. What is the meaning of the following in the Mul Mantra.
    (a) *Satnam*
    (b) *Ajuni Saibhang*
18. What does the word Nanak mean ?
19. What is the meaning of Sikh ?
20. Identify the following devotees of Guru Nanak:
    (a) He served him so well that he named him his successor
    (b) He became a devotee in his childhood and rose to the position of an important personage who performed the *tilak* ceremony of the next five Gurus.

B. WRITTEN

1. Write whether the following statements are True or False:
   (a) Guru Nanak founded Sikhism with the message of universal brotherhood.
   (b) Guru Nanak gave the Sikh salutation Sat Sri Akal.
   (c) Guru Nanak visited many religious places both of the Hindus and Muslims during his travels.
   (d) According to Guru Nanak, renunciation of worldly affairs is a way to salvation.
   (e) Guru Nanak preached that the God of Sikhs is different from the God of Hindus and Muslims.

2. Make a list of five teachings of Guru Nanak.

3. Which composition of Guru Nanak is recited everyday in the morning by devout Sikhs?

4. Write a paragraph of about 50 words explaining Guru Nanak's views on:
   (a) Superstitions
   (b) Vegetarianism

5. Write a *Sakhi* (story) of about 100 words to illustrate:
   (a) Learning without understanding is not good.
   (b) A mind wandering about worldly things cannot worship.
   (c) Never be greedy.
   (d) Good people are like fragrance that must scatter.
   (e) One should be kind even to animals.

6. Guru Nanak had spiritual learnings from his childhood. Write a story to illustrate this.

7. How did Guru Nanak reform Sajjan Thag ?

8. What did Guru Nanak do to persuade Hamza Gons to give up his fast ?

9. Besides the literal meaning of *tera*, it has a devotional significance in Sikhism. Write a story to illustrate this.

10. Guru Nanak was loved by both the Hindus and the Sikhs. What problems did it create at the time of Guru's passing away.

SAMPLE TEST PAPER

Time: 1 ½ hrs   Max Marks: 50

Instructions:
1. All questions are compulsory.
2. Marks for each question are indicated against it.

1. Answer the following in one word, phrase or sentence.
   (a) Which year will be the sixth birth centenary of Guru Nanak ?
   (b) Why was Guru Nanak not prepared to accept the sacred thread (*Janeiu*) as per the prevailing custom ?
   (c) What was the most significant event during Guru Nanak's stay at Sultanpur?
   (d) What message do you get from the *Sakhi* about Guru Nanak's visit to Mecca?
   (e) Why did Guru Nanak decline the invitation to a sumptuous dinner by Malik Bhago ?
   (f) Why did Salis Rai give Rs.100 for just looking at the diamond ?
   (g) Why did Guru Nanak feed the *sadhus* out of the money given to him by his father for trading ?
   (h) Where did Guru Nanak pass away ?   (8 X 2)

2. Write a paragraph of about 40 words about any one of the following values:
   (a) *Nam Japna*
   (b) *Kirat Karni*
   (c) *Wand Chhakna*   (4)

3. Write *sakhis* in about 80 words each about any *TWO* of the following :
   (a) Reforming a thief.
   (b) Encounter with the superstitious bathers at Hardwar.
   (c) Encounter with Wali Kandhari.   (8 X 2)

4. Write the complete life story of Guru Nanak in about 100 words bringing out the biographical details and two of his messages you consider most important.
                                                                        (14)

64